THE GOSLING

MARIAS RIVER FLOAT
MEMORIAL DAY WEEKEND
1993

POEMS

DAVID E. THOMAS

≈

BLUE HORSE PRESS REDONDO BEACH, CALIFORNIA 2017

THE GOSLING

MARIAS RIVER FLOAT
MEMORIAL DAY WEEKEND
1993

DAVID E. THOMAS

Blue Horse Press
318 Avenue I # 760
Redondo Beach,
California   90277

Cover art and all photos: Tim Irmen

Editors: Jeffrey and Tobi Alfier
Blue Horse Press logo: Amy Lynn Hayes

ISBN 978-0692904831

In memory

of

Frank Lloyd Sonnenberg

ACKNOWLEDGEMENTS

I would like to thank Jeff Alfier of Blue Horse Press for agreeing to publish this little book under his imprint and for his editorial work in its production. I would also like to thank my friend Tim Irmen for the use of his photographs and other assistance.

After twenty-four years I don't recall who all accompanied us on that float trip but everyone made some kind of contribution in terms of cooking or general information or momentary wit. Those I do recall are Bruce Carroll and Susie Goodman and their kids, Jess and Gabe, Jim Clayborn, the Kalispell artist, Frank Sonnenberg and his sons Chris and Max, Tim Irmen and then some co-workers with Jimmy Mitchell at the BLM, we made a lively crew and it was a good trip. Thanks to you all.

Contents

INTRODUCTION

The Marias River, so named by Meriwether Lewis
for a female acquaintance, arises from the confluence of
the Two Medicine River and Cut Bank Creek southeast of
Glacier National Park and meanders on a somewhat south
and easterly course until it flows into the Missouri River
near Loma, Montana, a small settlement north of Fort
Benton and Great Falls. Prior to the arrival of the Lewis
and Clark expedition in the area the Blackfeet and other
tribes roamed with the Blackfeet by far the dominant
group. One tribe, more easterly located, the Minnetares
referred to the Marias as "The River That Scolds All
Others" giving it a mythical component that the expedition
would find confusing in their search for an inland water
route to the Pacific Ocean. In the 1950's the river's course
was interrupted by the construction of Tiber Dam, taming
it somewhat but when the float trip described herein
occurred it was still a vibrant and scenic waterway and
continues to be to this day.

David E. Thomas

24 May 2017

ARRIVAL

Rain threat darkens
       the sky
Frank and I hike
        toward
the dam
an earthen
structure
with spillway
and north and south
outlet
channels formed
      of concrete
a road crowns
      the eminence
         we climb
wary
of rattlesnakes
the reservoir
Lake Elwell (named
for the longest serving
         district
judge in Montana history)
stretches
north and west
      looks low

the south outlet
roars with water
      drawn
from the depths of the Lake
the spillway dry
      but for a leak
the north outlet
      a quiet slough
home to three
      large
      carp
barely visible
in evening shadow.

28 May 1993

FIRST CAMP

I get my tent erect
        before the rain
comes
and the shuttle crew
           returns
not some NASA outfit
these guys
are flying close to the ground
        when they
        tumble out
Clayborn
crashes first
        the rest of us
        cluster
        around poached
           turkey breast
and mashed
potatoes
sipping whiskey
        and beer
rain drills

the big blue tarp
            a drumming
            resonance
beyond
campfire
lick and snap.

28 May 1993

FIRST LEG

We gathered last night
at Sanford campground
        below
        the dam
(Tiber Dam
A BuRec project of the 1950's
flood control/irrigation)
        old friends
and new all with Mitchell
        in common
the "commodore"
stayed the night
        explained
        the "charts"
but a death
in his family
leaves us lacking
        a certain
        commentary
a running geology lesson
on the particulars
        of the landforms
        we float by

(no Fleetwood Mac
on the boombox)
but we work our way
through head winds
            crosswinds
remembering how to read
            water
that lip of white curl
meaning rock
            "canoe eater"
the riffles that hint
            gravel bar
Tim and I are the blind
leading
the blind
            I've been
on this stretch before
but as a passenger
on the verge
            of sunstroke
mosquitoes sucking blood
by the quart now
            landscape
            appears
            familiar
yet foreign
a veneer

of anxiety coats
            my perception
all I really
            know
            is keep canoe
                        pointed
                        downriver
in search
of the island
that will be camp
(just a couple miles
            past Moffit bridge
Mitchell assured us at lunch
before driving off)
                        hard paddling
bend
after bend
            sore muscles
                        making
                        the proper
                                    channel
and we come ashore
to a good flat area
            dotted
with sagebrush
            and bunch grass

    the thunderheads

    which threatened

    all day

persist

towers of cloud

    high above

    cottonwoods

the wind

lifts the blue tarp

    we fashioned

    with some trouble

    into a tent

and Frank calls

    dinner

    "Coyote Stew"

29 May 1993

SECOND MORNING

Snores rip the night air
    A chorus
    of raw sound
like some momentous
        battle
        in the underworld
"This must scare the shit
        out of deer"
I lie thinking wishing
        for sleep
but sleep must've come
        because
        when I arise
        to piss
there's fog filtered
        dawn
light eerie gray all
        around
"Maybe I died
and went to San Francisco"
I think crawling
back into damp sleeping
        bag

a couple hours
and sun has burnt
    fog into tatters
Ron mixes pancake
   batter
on the camp stove
    coffee ready
one by one we emerge
blinking and stiff
    muscles
    seldom
    used
etch movement
with ache
  but the coffee
    works
pancakes
and sausage
  the tents come
    down
canoes loaded
and we're
on the water again.

30 May 1993

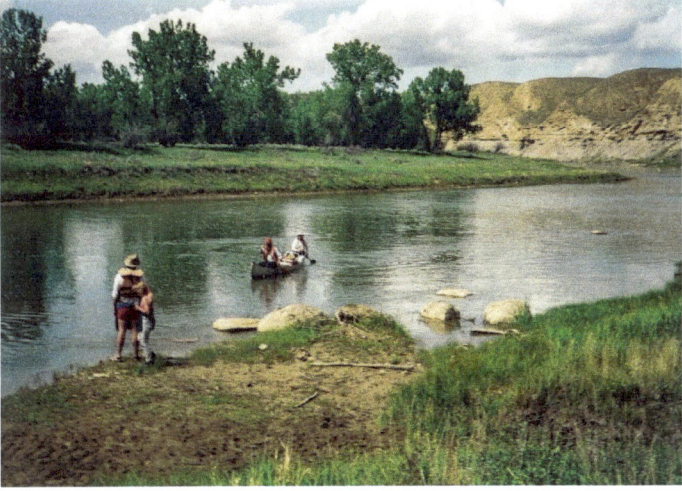

EAST FROM CIRCLE BRIDGE

After lunch
    Frank and I
float quiet
gnarly
cottonwood
    skeletons
         stark
against sagebrush ridge
morning cloud
        breaks
        into mid-day
sunlight
and shadows spread
        easy ripples
cloud
drama high
  in the atmosphere
nimbocumulus
      formations
      feeding
each other
tunnels of ice crystals
billowing
vast shapes

tempting
        dreams
but headwind
        develops
it's time
to paddle

II

piles of discarded
        baling twine
red and black
   laced
with pesticide
        herbicide
sliding down
        riverbank
"North Dakota fungus"
says Frank

III

we're passing through
        hoo-doo
land
sandstone erosions

                    stand
like desiccated
                    toadstools
along ridgelines
                    "hoo-doos"
a rookery
        of heron nests
in a cottonwood
                    snag
males
stand watch
        eggs wait
        to hatch

something challenging
        almost arrogant
        about this
                    vee
of Canada geese
                    flying
                    overhead
geese
in bankside reeds
stand
sentinel over
                    goslings
as we stroke by

IV

none of us are sure
        exactly
        when
or why
these five goslings
        began
        to follow
our flotilla
have they become lost?
were they abandoned?
        or emissaries
        from another world?
we have
clustered our canoes
        in slow water
        sharing beer
when the little geese
        appear
swimming
as easy as we walk
darting insect quick
        around
        the drifting canoes

and calling constantly
                their tiny cries
dull yellow down feathers
marked dark black billed
and black legged webbed
                      feet
they've been following
                for miles
in our wake
no more than a month
old not yet ready
                to fly
we urge them
into bankside reeds
                tall grass
hoping
the adults
we see circling above
will take them
                under wing
headwind grows
stiffer paddling
                harder
afternoon sun glare
makes shallows
and rocks
      hard to see

we run aground and life
                    gets a tad
                    grim
anxious
moments working
back into the deeper
                    channel
all the while moving
past table rocks
                    teetering
                    in mute defiance
past wind eroded
                    shapes inviting
the mind to dance
whole histories
swirl on a swallow's
                    wing
arms, necks, backs
aching
kids hungry, exhausted
                    a check
                    of the map
shows we've passed
                    our planned
                    camp

now the bank
near the battleship rock
            (or small aircraft
                        carrier perhaps)
looks like home
            and we pull in

                    V

home to a rattlesnake, too
            Roy quickly
            discovers
this narrow stretch
of tall grass
        sagebrush
                    and juniper
Clayborn
who hates snakes
                scoops it
up with a paddle
and hanging it over
                the water
walks down river
as it twists and strikes
it's out of venom
                when released
mad
but out
of our way

VI

sandstone cliff full
             of mud
             dauber
             swallow nests
rises above our tents
wind sculpted
             along the top
                         lower
some guy named R.F.
has drilled his initials
with a high powered rifle
from across the river

Mitchell's Penguin chili
takes on new ingredients
but retains
its original flavor
             we stand
             in the wind
             and eat
the chili
and quesadillas
             the dog Leroy
             discovers
             a peculiar thing
one lone gosling
of the original five

has climbed the bank
        stands chirping
        its young song
we coax it
back to the river
        hope adult
        geese will
        find it
and take charge

moon waxing full
        over wind
            spread cloud
swallows
chase evening insects

VII

raw pastels of sunset
        darken
evening star brightens
        campfire
        flames whip
        and flicker
lanterns lit
we drink beer
    and jabber
sip whiskey
and tell tales

lantern cast shadows
                on cliff face
the convexity
of its glass flue
        gives shadow
        a crisp edge
like walking in front
                of projector
during drive-in movie
intermission
those closest
to the burning mantels
                throw
the largest shadow
                we create
                our own
                cartoon show
moving fingers
                heads
                and camping objects
is this how ancient myth
developed?
In the midst of our goof
the gosling reappears

cold
frightened
it seeks comfort
attention
protection
Frank sticks it
in his coat
its song becomes
less shrill
glad of warmth
what are we to do
with this thing?
too small to eat
someone observes
we worry
about its getting
used
to human contact
why don't the adult geese
take care of it?
maybe we should take it
to Jarvis's duck farm
we make a nest
of paper towels
in a milk crate
try to feed it wet bread
Frank and Tim will shelter it
for the night
in their tent

VIII

near dawn bird calls
        awaken Frank
the gosling responds
        at first just
        a pheasant
but then a goose honks
        and the gosling
        sings back
Frank takes it to the water's
        edge
coaxes it into the reeds
it hesitates, he prods again
and it swims
        downstream
a couple hours later
        Roy reports
        an adult goose
        and three goslings
other side
of the river
during breakfast a formation
of Canada geese vees past
        honking
        down river

we load
canoes
a final time
    stroke by an eroded
    riverside hollow
fox hides
bright red fur
    against sandstone
waterfowl
easy hunting
        we fight
        stiff headwind
and are not sorry
to see the gauging station
        our autos
        parked close by

we leave the river
        through wheat fields
lone antelope grazes
        near Goosebill
          Hill
the Bear Paws
distant blue
in mid-day sun

so, too, the Sweetgrass Hills

30-31 May 1993

GREAT FALLS CODA

Giant Springs:
Canada geese float
      crystal
      water
with young
nearly ready
   to fly
   they chirp
   a song
we've come
to know
   rainbow trout
swim
the bright foliage
      below.

31 May 1993

About the Author

DAVID E. THOMAS grew up on the Hi-Line in North-central Montana. He graduated from the University of Montana then found himself on the streets of San Francisco where he began his literary education. Economic realities drove him to work on railroad gangs, big construction projects like Libby Dam and other labor intensive jobs. He has traveled in the United States, Mexico and Central America. He has published five books of poems, *Fossil Fuel, Buck's Last Wreck, The Hellgate Wind, Waterworks Hill* and *Old Power Company Road*. He has poems in the anthologies *The Last Best Place* and *Poems across the Big Sky I* and *II* and *New Poets of the American West* and has published poems in Romania, *Blue Collar Review, Cedilla 6, 7* and *8* and many other small magazines. His essay "Gothic Days" appears in *The Complete Montana Gothic* edited by Peter Koch which also features Thomas's earliest published work. Most recently he has published poems and an interview in *Talking River* and poems in *San Pedro River Review*. He lives in Missoula, Montana.